# HOW TO WRITE BETTER RESUMES IN
# 3 EASY STEPS

This book is written with **simplicity** in clear, concise, easy to read terminology. The authors' intention is to emphasize those **IMPORTANT BASIC FACTS** and show you how to write a **MORE EFFECTIVE RESUME** in a simple format that is **EASIER FOR THE EMPLOYER TO READ.** The express purpose is to help you make a **GOOD FIRST IMPRESSION** to ensure the employer will read your total resume. All this in fifty pages PLUS a computer disk for your personal computer with resume formats, and cover letter formats. Good luck in your job search.

Ben T. Field

Paul K. Wright

# BETTER RESUMES IN 3 EASY STEPS

By Ben T. Field &
Paul K. Wright
(Revised & enlarged)

This publication is designed to provide accurate and authoritative information in regard to the subject matter covered. It is sold with the understanding that neither the publisher nor the author is engaged in rendering legal, accounting, or other professional advice, service or consultation. If legal advice or other expert assistance is required, the services of a competent professional should be sought.

*From a Declaration of Principles jointly adopted by a committee of the American Bar Association and a committee of publishers.*

# Table of Contents

# Introduction

The authors recognize there are many good books on the market about how to write resumes showing the different types of resumes, with virtually thousands of examples.

They contain an incredible amount of information with many good points to help you in your job search. However, having so much information has also caused some confusion among many applicants. This book was written to alleviate some of that confusion and make it easier to write an effective resume . . . that the employer will read . . . complete with a disk for your computer.

*Only 50 pages to read*

Moreover, the workplace has changed drastically during the last decade. Hiring practices have changed even more. The authors of this monograph have a combined knowledge of over fifty years experience dealing with company practices and have seen those changes taking place.

We have reviewed numerous resumes in the past ten years and many resume books during that time with examples of how to write resumes from the "outstanding" resume to the "best" resume that will get you the job you want, but . . .

*SOURCE: Scripps Howard News Service

David Bowman, Founder of Kinko's Service Corp. recently said the average time a manager took to scan a resume was **TWENTY SECONDS*** to determine if the applicant should be granted an interview. He also stressed good format and accomplishments. Think about this impact on your resume.

*Remember this! Only 20 seconds or less*

Richard Gaither, nationally known Job Search Consultant and Author, said that you only have 7 seconds. Many employers scan the resume looking for one particular item they want while others look for something they don't want.

This means you **must** get the employer's attention immediately. You must have an **outstanding** resume not only in what it says, but how it says it, plus a **professional appearance**.

*You must generate interest*

It's like the Townsend system of advertising . . . AIDMA . . .
attract ATTENTION,
generate INTEREST,
create DESIRE,
establish MEMORY,
stimulate ACTION - but you must do this in only **TWENTY SECONDS**.

This book is written to show you how to make your resume **more effective** and how to get that attention in the first **TWENTY SECONDS**.

*Read every page*

2

# The Changing Workplace

The workplace is more competitive and complex than ever before. Companies continue to downsize their operations and reduce their workforce. Consequently, you must now compete with experienced workers looking for employment as well as the new college graduate.

Even though workers have been considered to be the company's most valuable resource, they become expendable when the company is reducing operating costs. Therefore, when you now apply for a position, the company **wants to know what you have accomplished** in an effort to determine your potential value.

The advice we offer in this book will help you fine-tune your resume to make it more professional, more dynamic, and more effective to compete in today's market. Most managers use the **process of elimination** when looking at resumes whether or not they realize or admit it. It's almost like a beauty contest and you are one of the contestants. You must make a good impression **immediately.**

**Or you may be eliminated before they consider your experience.**

Most beauty contests have three phases. 1 - the bathing suit competition. 2 - the evening gown competition and 3 - the intellectual question. Think about it, and remember what David Bowman said about the first twenty seconds.

The **first glance** considers the appearance, that makes it stand out from the rest. The **second glance** considers the content, your profile, your skills. The **final glance** the details, to determine your potential with the company. In other words, you must attract the reader's attention and generate his interest in **TWENTY SECONDS** or you won't have the opportunity to prove your intellect.

We will explain on the following pages the use of key words, action verbs, and the most usable format with step by step instructions. We advise you not to worry about the various types of resumes such as functional or chronological. Simply follow our examples with necessary variations to emphasize your strengths and make your resume more effective.

**Make it easy for the employer to read.**

*You must make a good impression in 20 seconds!*

*A neat simple layout is easiest to read*

# The Resume. Its Purpose and Format

The resume is a document that shows the employer your assets and liabilities, your strengths and weaknesses; what you have done and what you can do for the employer. It is your personal sales presentation about you and your capabilities. Most of all, it is your personal advocate to **gain you an interview.**

It won't get you the job, but a good resume will get your foot in the door. The rest is up to you. Therefore, it is extremely important for your resume to be **factual and professional.** But, it must accentuate the positive and eliminate the negative as much as possible.

You will note that our resume examples show a **professional profile** or **summary** rather than an objective. In some cases when applicable, you might use **special qualifications.**

This will emphasize your strong points immediately and encourage the manager to read further, rather than limit consideration to a specific job. However as we will explain later, **a new graduate right out of college should combine a career objective with the profile.** Please pay careful attention to our instructions about how to write it.

You have usually mentioned your goal in your cover letter or your interest in the company's job opening.

**So, if you feel that you must document a particular objective, then add it to the profile as shown in the examples:**

*Extensive experience in human resources and administrative procedures, supporting top management. Looking for similar position in administrative or systems capacity.*

OR

*Ten years experience in computer programming, operations and maintenance, including systems analysis and design. Looking for similar position in healthcare or related field.*

**How long should a resume be?** A one-page resume is the best and the most acceptable. In most cases you can get all the important information on one page. A survey last year of executives in the nations 1,000 largest firms reported that 73% preferred one page for staff-level positions but 64% preferred two pages for executive positions. However, in cases where you have so much experience (such as technical) that you must use two pages, it is mandatory to capture the readers interest on the first page to insure he/she will read the second page.

Therefore, we recommend that a two-page resume be a double-page spread printed on 11 X 17 paper folded to 8 1/2 X 11 so the reader is forced to see both pages when the resume is opened as shown later in the examples. Be sure to put your name and address on the front in case the employer files your resume for future reference . . . but . . .
if you use the two pages in lieu of the double page spread, staple them so they won't get separated. Use only the straight style staples, and not undulated.

*you must present facts*

*one page is best if you want her*

# Key Components That Attract Attention

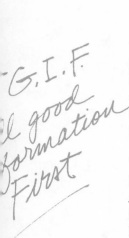

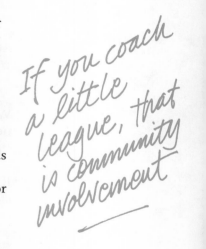

You will note that we recommend a simple, straight-forward, eye-catching format with **dynamic** headings. This will emphasize the most important factors first.

Therefore, begin with the **PROFILE, SKILLS,** and **ACCOMPLISHMENTS.** Even if you are just out of college, you have skills and accomplishments from college that will generate the employers interest.

It is true that some employers like to see a career objective. But remember, this may limit you being considered for various positions whereas a profile covers a broader range. **So add the objective to the profile like the example on the opposite page.**

We continue to stress the importance of a PROFILE followed by SKILLS & ABILITIES and/or ACCOMPLISHMENTS to enhance your value to the employer. **Accomplishments impress people** and this is your opportunity to sell yourself! Use action words to your best advantage.

Remember, you must make a good impression in **TWENTY SECONDS.** If you have special qualifications, by all means show them, especially if you can't show accomplishments.

BASIC FORMAT
PROFILE
SKILLS & ABILITIES
ACCOMPLISHMENTS
WORK EXPERIENCE
RELATED TRAINING
EDUCATION
CERTIFICATION
(or AFFILIATIONS)

Depending on the kind of position, you may need to add the heading for COMMUNITY (or civic) INVOLVEMENT. Many employers require middle management personnel to be active in the community and want to know if you worked on fund drives (hospitals, United Way, etc.), Chamber of Commerce committees, or served on boards of directors. They do not care about your hobbies, interests, or sports.

**BASIC FORMAT (College Students or New Graduate)**
You can still use this format, but it will have to be structured to emphasize your education and training plus any work experience or activities during college. For example, your PROFILE could read like this, **"Motivated college graduate with training in computer technology and above average math scores pursuing a career in systems analysis."** But **don't** embellish how much value you can be to the company right out of college with no experience. Do not antagonize the employer's intelligence.

5

# Basic Resume Outline
**(Easy To Read)**

Name
Address
City State Zip
Phone

**PROFILE (or SUMMARY):** This is your sales presentation. It outlines your experience in a nutshell. Remember - you are a sophisticated product that must be marketed.

**SKILLS & ABILITIES or QUALIFICATIONS:** If applicable. (see pp 11-12-13).

**ACCOMPLISHMENTS:** Be specific, such as, you increased sales by 100%, reduced operation costs by 30%, etc. (see pp 7 & 10)

**WORK EXPERIENCE:** Show company, location, title, responsibilities, brief explanation and terms of employment.

**RELATED TRAINING:** Any company training, continuing education classes, seminars, workshops, etc.

**EDUCATION:** Postsecondary education with field of study, degree or certificate.

**COMMUNITY INVOLVEMENT** (whenever applicable) Fund drives, committees, board of directors, and offices held.

**CERTIFICATION** (whenever applicable)

**AFFILIATIONS** (whenever applicable)

**Note: The popular phrase "References furnished on request" is not necessary.**

# Compile Your Information

## Step One

OR

You are now ready either to evaluate and revise your current resume to improve it or write a new one. **The first step is to compile complete information** about you - your skills, your training, your accomplishments, community involvement, everything you can think of.

Begin with your work experience. List every company, location, and dates of employment. For each company, note every job you held, everything you did, your duties and responsibilities, your accomplishments and any awards. List all your skills, tools and equipment used, and all company training. List any outside activities the company required you to do, such as fund drives, committees, boards of directors, etc.

**Now, pick out your strong points** that apply to the job group or job opening you are seeking, so you can write an action-packed **PROFILE**. For example, you could say . . .

*Fifteen years in bank management, including extensive commercial lending and ten years in charge of the Mortgage Loan Department.*

*Broad-based experience in consumer product design including injection molded and vacuum-formed plastic parts. Also designed product packaging, displays , and in-plant fixtures.*

The **PROFILE** is the first item the employer will read after the name and address. It is the first part of your sales presentation. You must generate interest in the first few seconds, so he/she will continue.

**Next, pick out your most impressive ACCOMPLISHMENTS.** This is the second part of your sales presentation to generate his/her interest. Be specific and use action words. For example . . .

*Increased annual refrigerator sales by 100% from $500,000 to $1,000,000.*

*Reduced delinquent accounts by 35% in one year.*

**Finally, review all training related to your work experience** with emphasis on training that would apply to the job opening or job group you are seeking.

*The Profile generates the first impression. Make it good!*

*Accomplishments impress people*

*SCANS skills will enhance your resume*

## REFER TO THE SCANS SKILLS, page 11

| FOUNDATION SKILLS | COMPETENCIES |
|---|---|
| • Basic Skills | • Resources |
| • Thinking Skills | • Information |
| • Personal Qualities | • Interpersonal |
| | • Systems |
| | • Technology |

# Employment Worksheet

List every company, location, job, and term of employment. On the following pages we will show you how to emphasize the major employers and accentuate that work experience to your best advantage.

Company _____ City _____

Job Title _____ from _____ to _____

Job Description _____

_____

_____

_____

_____

_____

_____


Company _____ City _____

Job Title _____ from _____ to _____

Job Description _____

_____

_____

_____

_____

_____

_____


Company _____ City _____

Job Title _____ from _____ to _____

Job Description _____

_____

_____

_____

_____


Company _____ City _____

Job Title _____ from _____ to _____

Job Description _____

_____

_____

_____

_____

# Education & Training Worksheet

List every educational institution, location, studies, diplomas, certificates, or degree attained, graduation date, etc.

High School _____ From _____ To _____

City and state _____ Graduation date _____

Major studies _____ Diploma _____

_____

Technical school _____ From _____ To _____

City and state _____ Graduation date _____

Major studies _____ Certificate _____

_____

College/University _____ From _____ To _____

City and state _____ Graduation date _____

Major studies _____ Degree _____

_____

College/University _____ From _____ To _____

City and state _____ Graduation date _____

Major studies _____ Degree _____

_____

Additional training or college courses _____

School _____ From _____ To _____

Subject _____ Certificate _____

Explain _____

_____

School _____ From _____ To _____

Subject _____ Certificate _____

Explain_____

Make a list of other work-related training or company sponsored seminars, workshops, etc. Show subject, sponsor, location and dates.

# Analyze Your Information and Evaluate Your Skills

## Step Two

You have compiled information about each job you held, everything you did and everything you accomplished. Now, you **must evaluate the data** to determine what is most valuable or useful to the employer who reads your resume.

You must **FOCUS on what experiences would be most relevant and important** to your new employer and emphasize them accordingly.

*Emphasize the facts most relevant to the new position*

You must also determine your **most important accomplishments** that would show your potential value in your new position.

Many of the things that you did during your work experience are no longer important, especially if you have advanced during your .employment and are applying for a better position. The past is over so you must summarize your experience in each job accordingly as we will show in the examples. Emphasize skills and experiences that are important to the new employer.

Evaluate the information and its relevancy to the SCANS Skills that are explained on the following pages.

Remember that **accomplishments impress people**. We mentioned previously that the employer wants to know what you did in order to determine your potential value to his/her company. Therefore, we must repeat that "ACCOMPLISHMENTS" is a key part of your sales presentation to generate interest in you. **Select your most impressive accomplishments** and document them as much as possible with details about what you accomplished, such as,

*Increased sales by 50% from $100,000 to $150,000*

*Reduced delinquent accounts by 35%, in one year.*

The action words on page 14 will help you in summarizing your experiences and your accomplishments.

Many experts say it is not necessary to show experience past ten years but if it can be done without too much verbiage, we recommend that you at least compile your experience for a twenty year period and use whatever is applicable. In most cases you can detail the recent ten to fifteen years and summarize the previous experiences as shown in the example resumes.

# SCANS Report and Skills For The Future

Today's workplace is changing so rapidly the authors feel that it is necessary to explain the SCANS* report which deals with skills that employers look for in new employees. Both entry level and experienced job seekers are affected. Every recent survey emphasizes the importance of these skills so the SCANS Report has a definite impact on how you write your resume, what you say, and how you say it.

Even though you may have the basic foundation skills of reading, writing, math, listening and speaking-employers want to know how well you can communicate both orally and in writing. They want to know how well you organize information and respond to instructions, how well you solve problems and work with others. In other words, in today's workplace, you must demonstrate critical think-ing, problem solving, and the popular term of interacting - being a team player or a team leader.

**The way you write your resume will show the employer how well you organize information, how well you think, and how responsible you are.**

The point here is to be very careful what you say and how you say it.

How you write your PROFILE, your SKILLS, ACCOMPLISHMENTS and your WORK EXPERIENCE will demonstrate these skills.

For your information, the SCANS report listed the **five competencies** as follows:

**RESOURCES** - How well do you organize your time, plan your work, and utilize available resources?

**INFORMATION** - How well do you acquire, evaluate, organize, interpret, and communicate informa-tion? Are you computer literate?

**INTERPERSONAL** - How well do you work with others, serve clients, and exercise leadership? Teamwork?

**SYSTEMS** - How well do you understand social, organization, and technological systems?

**TECHNOLOGY** - How well do you select and apply technology in your work?

The **three foundation skills** are basic skills, thinking skills and personal qualities as follows:

**BASIC SKILLS** - include reading, writing, math, listening, and speak-ing.

**THINKING SKILLS** - include crea-tive thinking, decision making, problem solving, visualizing, knowing how to learn, and reason.

**PERSONAL QUALITIES** - include responsibility, sociability, self-management, integrity and honesty.

*These skills are mandatory in the workplace today.*

* Secretary's Commission on Achieving Necessary Skills, U.S. Department of Labor, April 1992

Keep these facts in mind when you describe your work experience, job responsibilities and your accomplishments. Your resume must convince the employer that you have these important skills.

# Enhance Your Resume With SCANS Skills

Remember that you are selling your-self to the employer and the resume is your sales presentation that you have the job skills he/she wants.

But you also need to enhance your resume with the SCANS skills. These are basic skills that employers expect every employee to have in addition to the specific skills relative to the job.

The same three steps used in writing a resume apply to using SCANS skills in your resume.

1. **Compile** all the skills you believe you have

2. **Analyze** those skills for relative importance, and

3. **Organize** them according to the order that it appears the new employ-er wants. You can then decide which skills should be woven into the profile and which ones should domi-nate the section under "SKILLS & ABILITIES" along with job specific skills.

Study the SCANS skills on the pre-ceding page and see how they are presented in the following examples:

In the PROFILE

"Degreed engineer with project management expertise in construction with proven experience in problem-solving and a track record of complet-ing projects on time."

And under ACCOMPLISHMENTS

"Completed multi-million dollar 100 home subdivision 5% under budget in one year."

Using SCANS skills in your resume will make it stand out above the rest. They will impress the employer that you have the foundation skills and the competencies that are mandatory in todays' workplace.

Here are some examples of what you might emphasize under the SKILLS & ABILITIES heading:

- Excellent communication skills (oral and written)
- Excellent interpersonal skills (teamwork)
- Proven interpersonal skills (working with management/staff)
- Proven analytical and problem-solving skills and detail oriented
- Proficient computer skills
- Ability to organize and implement projects
- Ability to interpret and implement federal regulations
- Self starter, motivated and dedicated worker

*Make it factual— you may have to prove it*

However, remember that if you say you have excellent communication skills or interpersonal skills in lieu of good skills, or proficient, etc., make sure you do and be prepared to explain how in the interview. A study by (Michigan State University) College Employment Research Institute last year reported that good communication skills were among the most important attributes of suc-cessful applicants, and also the most notable deficiencies in new college graduates.

Now, before you begin Step Three to write your PROFILE, your SKILLS & ABILITIES, etc., review the infor-mation on the preceding page to determine your strong points that you can emphasize.

# Skills & Accomplishments Worksheet

List all skills and accomplishments for each job held. Use extra paper if you need more space. Don't be bashful. List everything you can.

Company_____City_____
Job Title_____From_____To_____
What you did_____
_____
Accomplishments_____
_____

_____
_____
_____

Company_____City_____
Job Title_____From_____To_____
What you did_____
_____
Accomplishments_____
_____

_____
_____
_____

Company_____City_____
Job Title_____From_____To_____
What you did_____
_____
Accomplishments_____
_____

_____
_____
_____

Company_____City_____
Job Title_____From_____To_____
What you did_____
_____
Accomplishments_____
_____

_____
_____
_____

# Use Action Words & Phrases

Now that you have compiled complete information about everything you ever did - your responsibilities and your achievements, you must summarize your experience under each of the headings - your PROFILE, your ACCOMPLISHMENTS, your WORK EXPERIENCE, etc. Use action words to emphasize what you accomplished, indicating your capabilities. The following list will give you examples of words that will enhance your resume.

- accomplished
- achieved
  administered
  analyzed
  approved
  assisted
- attained
- completed
  conducted
  coordinated
- created
  demonstrated
- designed
  determined
- developed
  directed
- established
  evaluated
  generated
  handled
  implemented
- improved

- increased
  initiated
  instituted
  introduced
- invented
- maintained
- managed
- negotiated
  operated
- organized
- originated
  planned
  prepared
  presented
- prevented
- produced
- proved
  provided
- rectified
  recommended
- reduced
- replaced
  reviewed
  revised
- saved
- simplified
- succeeded
  supported
- supervised
  trained
  validated
  verified

> *All of these words denote action but those indicated by a center dot • denote accomplishment and should be used where they fit best. Many of them have been used in the example resumes.*

**Note:** When applicable, you may want to use such phrases as "in charge of", "responsible for", "skilled in", "proven accomplishments in", "proven track record in", "extensive experience in". "broad-based experience in", etc.

# Be Creative But Don't Be Stupid

Most resume books on the market tell you to be creative. This is true to a certain extent and you must use your initiative. But "don't be stupid" and make a bad impression in the first twenty seconds.

The **first impression is like a parachute jump.** You only have one chance to survive.

Here are several examples but we will discuss other mistakes and errors under the appropriate subjects later in this book.

**PAPER** - many authors tell you to use colors that stand out. Good idea but think first. We received about one hundred resumes recently in response to an ad and several stood out. One was on red paper. We could hardly see the printing. One on beautiful parchment and printed in old English typeface. One on a cheap paper in script we couldn't read at all. In fact, we didn't.

For example, you can paint a cow purple to make her stand out from the herd, but who wants a purple cow? Bullfighters use a red cape to antagonize the bull. Get the point? We'll discuss paper and color later.

**TYPE** - as we pointed out in the previous paragraph, resumes must be neat and readable. If you were applying to a particular artistic company that dealt with that kind of design work, then maybe something like Old English on parchment might be appropriate. But never under normal circumstances should you use a typeface that is difficult to read.

**OBJECTIVES - one of the most blatant mistakes on resumes is for the applicant to assume his/her value to the employer** under an OBJECTIVE heading with statements like - "looking for a rewarding position that will use my management/administrative skills for the benefit of the company" or "progressive organization that will utilize my experience while offering opportunity for advancement" or "use my interpersonal skills and education in a professional setting" or "utilize my talents and management skills to improve company operations" etc.

Be creative in selling your capabilities. But **"don't be stupid"** in telling the employer about your value to him. **Over-selling can be as detrimental as under-selling.** However, remember what Elmer Wheeler said. Sell the sizzle, not the steak. Emphasize your accomplishments so the **employer can determine** your value to the firm and how you may be an asset.

**FORMAT** - Start with the simple format explained on pages 5 & 6 if you want to generate interest A.S.A.P.... That also means:
APPEARANCE
STRUCTURE
ACCOMPLISHMENTS
PROOF.
The rest is history.

*this will make or break your first impression*

*Be careful what you say and how you say it.*

15

# Organize Your Information

## Step Three

You are now ready to write or rewrite your resume. Use the following outline as a worksheet and make notations. Examples are on the following pages.

Most experts recommend your name, address, city, state, zip code and phone number be centered at the top of the page. Put your name in bold. There is an acceptable alternate heading shown in the examples used when space is limited

---

**Your Name**
Your Address
Your City, State, Zip Code
Your Phone Number

*Nice appearance and easy to read*

PROFILE or PROFESSIONAL PROFILE, etc.
(in case of new graduate, add Career Objective)

SKILLS & ABILITIES or QUALIFICATIONS, etc. (if applicable)

ACCOMPLISHMENTS or SELECTED ACCOMPLISHMENTS

WORK EXPERIENCE or PROFESSIONAL EXPERIENCE

RELATED TRAINING

*Keep it simple!*

EDUCATION or EDUCATION & TRAINING

COMMUNITY INVOLVEMENT (if applicable)

CERTIFICATIONS (if applicable)

AFFILIATIONS (if applicable, such as Engineering groups, etc.)

NOTE: If you can't show any ACCOMPLISHMENTS, at least show SPECIAL SKILLS or QUALIFICATIONS, etc.

# Profile or Faux pas?

Many things people put on resumes or leave off resumes may not actually be mistakes or errors, but they could easily be called a faux pas. They can affect your resume in a negative manner.

Many of the Do's and Don'ts are covered on the following page but some of the most common errors are found in statements such as:

**"Seeking entry-level position"**
Don't tell the employer you want an entry-level position. You are placing a limit on yourself and influencing his first impression. He may have other plans, such as management training, etc., but you just blew it.

**"Seeking full-time employment"**
This is superfluous and doesn't tell the employer anything. It's similar to the statement that you will take any job available. Employers want you to have some kind of direction.

**"Seeking position that will utilize my creative and promotional skills to improve the company's operation."** You are telling the employer that you know more about the company than he does.

**"Seeking entry-level position with established company which rewards hard work with increasing responsibilities and management roles."** This is superfluous because employers normally reward (hard) work with responsibilities provided the employee is capable and does good work.

**"Seeking rewarding position that will fully utilize my personal and professional experience."** This is completely superfluous because the employer will fully utilize your experience if you put forth the effort.

**"Seeking challenging position where I can use and contribute my education and job experience"** The phrase *challenging position* is overworked and doesn't mean anything. The addition of contributing your education and job experience is something the employer already expects from you so you haven't generated any interest on his part.

**"Seeking position that offers career potential"** Also overworked, meaningless and doesn't tell the employer anything.

Another common error is the number of pages. We explained the use of one-page and two-page resumes, but invariably some applicant will write several pages about work experiences, include a full-page of references, copies of awards, transcripts and other material. **Don't do it!** If the employer wants a complete portfolio, he/she will ask for it.

Also do not include your salary history as part of your resume. It's a calculated risk even when the employer requests it. Suggestions on how to handle the request for salary history or salary requirement are included in our book "Better Job Search In 3 Easy Steps".

# Do's and Don'ts That Are Critical

### Do's

• Make sure you have a nice, neat layout. One that is pleasing to the eye with enough border and white space to emphasize your resume so it won't look like a newspaper ad.

• Use a nice, neat easy-to-read type-face on good, quality bond paper as discussed later.

• Use matching envelopes if at all possible.

• Use the strong outline format we suggest. This makes it easy for the employer to scan your resume quickly. **Remember the critical first 20 Seconds.** In fact, Richard Gaither (author and consultant) said you may only have seven to ten seconds.

• Emphasize and document your accomplishments with specific results.

• Use the most appropriate action-words to emphasize your accomplishments.

• Be sure to show college graduation dates, location of school, and degree.

• Always include a cover letter with your resume.

• Make sure your cover letter is neatly typed to match your resume.

• Use your real name.

### Don'ts

• Don't clutter the resume page like a newspaper ad and don't use too large a typeface.

• Don't use script or fancy, hard-to-read typefaces.

• Don't use cute or novel ways to organize your resume. Stay with the simple format recommended by experts.

• Don't leave gaps in your employment history.

• Don't include personal information about age, health or marital status. It's not necessary and could be detrimental to you.

• Don't include anything about hobbies, sports, interests, etc.

• Don't mention religious or political affiliations unless you are applying for those kinds of jobs.

• Don't refer to wages or salaries.

• Don't use terms like *fired, laid off* or other derogatory words.

• Don't date your resume but you should update it periodically.

• Don't hand-write your resume or cover letter.

• Don't use your nickname, such as Jimmy, Billy, Suzy, Joey, Billy Joe, etc.

# Paper Quality, Color, Typefaces & More

The appearance of your resume is critical. It must be pleasing to the eye to ensure the employer will read it. Pay attention to every detail: paper, quality, color, typeface, layout, printing. Everything is important.

We suggest that, if at all possible, you have it printed at a commercial printer. However, if you have a good master copy, use good quality paper, and have access to a good copy machine, those copies are usually acceptable.

**PAPER** should be top quality. A good heavy bond paper, possibly with a linen finish and 25% rag content. Try to use 24 lb. paper. Any lighter weight like 20 lb. may be too flimsy and won't have the quality and feel you need.

**PAPER COLOR** should be pleasing to your eyes. The best colors are white, ivory, buff, sand (tan), or gray. Never use harsh colors like red, blue, green, or other colors that are too dark, making your resume difficult to read.

**TYPEFACES** must be easy to read. Typefaces like Times Roman, Caslon, Baskerville, or Garamond will always be in good taste. Should you want a more modern, contemporary look, choose a typeface like Helvetica, Futura, Optima or Univers. Typefaces like Old English, Brush, Script, or other fancy styles should never be used in your resume. **Never mix your typefaces.** It is OK to use regular, bold, and italics of the same face in different sizes for emphasis but don't use a serif type and sans-serif type in the same resume.

**PRINTING** is best done at a commercial printer. Many independent printers, like PIP or Kinko's etc., are relatively inexpensive. If you have a master copy from a laser printer, they can use it as camera ready copy. Many printers can set your type and do the complete job. But you must give them typewritten copy exactly the way it should be. Then you have to proof-read to make sure everything looks the way it should.

**LAYOUT** is very important. It must present your resume in the best possible way. White space at top, bottom and both sides will give the best appearance and impression. Remember the old adage that the white space sells the content. Look closely at the resume examples in this book and you'll see what we mean. **Watch your layout.**

**ENVELOPES** are an important part of your resume package. Use matching envelopes if at all possible. If not, blend as close to your stationery as you can. Use a regular business size (No. 10) envelope for 1-page or 2-page resumes with a cover letter. But if you use the 11 X 17 double page spread format (folded to 8 1/2 X 11) use a 9 X 12 booklet style envelope. This way, neither your resume, nor your cover letter will have to be folded. **Looks are everything.**

**Note:** If you are using a pin-dot printer, you will not get a choice of typefaces or letter quality output like an ink-jet or laser printer gives you. Find someplace that can print your resume so it will have the best appearance possible. You always want to make the best impression possible on a future employer.

*e high quality paper a good impression*

*IMPORTANT! must be easy to read*

*White space gives your resume the professional look!*

*you must use a good printer!*

19

# What Do Employers Expect?
## Does your resume sell your skills?
## Will it pass the tests?

### A Quick Review

Numerous surveys about what employers expect in employees have been published in the last few years. Virtually all of them reached similar conclusions. Employers of the nineties want employees to have better skills to meet the demands of the high-performance technological workplace.

These skills were identified in the U.S. Department of Labor 1992 SCANS Report as the **Foundation Skills and the five Workplace Competencies** (Review page 11).

Unfortunately, many applicants, including young people entering the workforce do not possess these skills.

Therefore, applicants that do possess these skills stand out way above the rest. It is important for you to show them on your resume to impress the employer.

You can easily prove you have BASIC skills and THINKING skills by the appearance and content of your resume (Page 12). What you say will also reflect PERSONAL QUALITIES. How you explain your work experience and job responsibilities will reflect your WORKPLACE COMPETENCIES.

Employers expect you to have the **Foundation Skills** and as many **Competencies** as relevant, so make your resume show them.

Remember, if you impress the employers, they **will** read your resume. If you sell your skills, they **will** call you in for an interview.

### Test #1: Critical Factors

Will your resume pass the three critical factors test to achieve a good impression? Does it have:
**1** -A pleasing appearance (easy to read). **2** - Good qualifications ( your profile). **3** - Proof of ability (your skills & accomplishments)

### Test #2: Workplace Competencies
Will your resume pass the Competencies test?

**First** - check the **appearance** factor. This will identify your BASIC skills of reading, writing and speaking, and your INFORMATION competency of organizing data.

**Second** - check your **profile** factor. This will identify many qualifications including BASIC skills in writing, THINKING skills, PERSONAL QUALITIES, and several competencies including INTERPERSONAL skills, INFORMATION skills, and TECHNOLOGY skills.

**Third** - check your PROOF of ABILITY factor. This is very critical because it may or may not prove that you have the qualifications you said you have. Factual accomplishments and/or skills prove that you have all the BASIC skills, all the THINKING skills, the PERSONAL QUALITIES, and most of the competencies.

**Remember** - The Michigan State University Study (page 12) reported that good communication skills were among the most important attributes of new employees.

# Critical Factors & Personal Marketing

## This is it! You have 20 seconds or less!

You must make a good impression immediately! You only have one chance and a few seconds to make a good first impression.

**The first critical factor** is the appearance. If the resume appearance is not pleasing, you may be eliminated before the employer even reads your name.

**The second critical factor** is your profile. This is your sales presentation. You are marketing your experience and capabilities. Make it good but make it factual - it is a summary of your assets.

**The third critical factor** for a good impression is your accomplishments ( and/or skills ) which prove what you said. We repeat that **accomplishments impress people.** They will make the potential employer believe you can be valuable to the company far more than you telling how valuable you can be.

### EFFECTIVENESS

We recommend only two styles for an effective resume that the employer will read. One page is sufficient for most resumes but if you must use two pages, then use the double page spread shown below. This will ensure the employer will see **both pages** upon opening the resume, whereas the second page of a two-page resume will often be overlooked

### K.I.S.S. - You're in the 90's now!

Keep it short and simple so the employer will read your resume and grant you an interview . . . BUT . . . be specific about what you can do and thorough about what you have done. Employers in the 90's receive hundreds and thousands of resumes every year. They don't have the time to read them all so they read the best and eliminate the rest.

**Remember the three most important factors to make that first impression good:**

**1)** PLEASING APPEARANCE with a simple format that's **easy to read.**

**2)** GOOD QUALIFICATIONS (your profile) that will attract the employers **attention.**

**3)** PROOF OF ABILITY - your accomplishments and/or skills. **You said it, so now you have to prove it.**

*A.S.AP. means Appearance Structure Accomplishments Proof*

Best way . . one page.

But . . . if you must have two pages then use the double page spread with your name centered on the front.

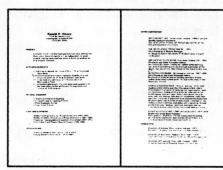

11 X 17 folded to 8 1/2 X 11 with name and address on front. Mail with cover letter, flat in 9 X 12 heavy envelope.

*Nice neat layout - easy to read*

# IMAJEAN WADE
6720 SUNSET PIKE
LOUISVILLE, KY 40291
Phone: 502-473-6467

## PROFILE
Human Resources professional with extensive experience in adminis trative procedures, supporting top management. Looking for similar position in administrative or systems capacity

## SKILLS & ABILITIES
*SCANS skills*

- Excellent communication and customer relations skills
- Team player with excellent interpersonal skills
- Proven organizational, negotiation, and leadership skills
- Proven critical thinking and problem-solving skills
- Motivated self-starter and detail oriented
- Proficient computer skills including mainframe manipulation

## PROFESSIONAL EXPERIENCE
1990 - 1993:      **ALCO INDUSTRIES**          Louisville, Kentucky
**EIS SYSTEMS ADMINISTATOR**
MANAGED and CONTROLLED salary administration and personnel records for 1,100 salaried employees.
ADMINISTERED supplementary pay for 400 production supervisors in addition to previous responsibilities listed below.

*Very factual*

1980 - 1990:      **ALCO INDUSTRIES**          Louisville, Kentucky
**SENIOR ADMINISTRATIVE ASSISTANT**
PREPARED salaried employees' job descriptions and maintained salaried personnel performance audits, career paths, and professional profile information.
PERFORMED administrative duties in labor relations, benefits, training and employee assistance program.
ADMINISTERED (25-year) awards program and made travel arrangements (including conference meeting rooms) for Human Resources Director and staff

## EDUCATION & TRAINING
Louisville Business College, Louisville, KY 1979
University of Louisville, Louisville, KY 1981 - 1985.
(Evening classes, business law, BASIC programming)

*All of these examples are actual resumes that got results.*

*Except pages 23 and 25 that show what not to do !*

*Nice appearance, but no facts.*

*This is a very ineffective resume!*

## William D. Brown
41 Westwood Drive
Atlanta, GA 40296
609-453-3198

### JOB OBJECTIVE
Seeking full-time employment.

*Superflous objective with no meaning*

### EDUCATION
1980    Advanced degree in Counseling
        Georgia Tech University, Atlanta GA
1973    Masters Degree in Art
        Murray State University, Murray KY
1970    Bachelor of Science Degree in Art
        Murray State University, Murray KY

### SKILLS & ABILITIES
**Leadership:** Created innovative programs for youth and adults
to help them make successful choices in education and/or careers,
including counseling and guidance.

**Communication:** Excellent oral and written communication
skills reinforced by twenty years experience counseling students regarding scholarships, colleges, universities, technical schools, careers and
employment. Exemplified by school admissions and job placement.

**Artistic:** Proven ability in commercial art backed up with both
Bachelors Degree and Masters Degree in art.

• References available on request •

*No proof of work history*

*No proof of skills or abilities*

# CHARLES E. WIGGER

8120 Woodbriar Drive
Evansville, Indiana 47715
(812) 477-4110

*Good profile!*

## PROFILE

Diversified mechanic with broad-based experience in heavy equipment, truck driving and maintenance plus a technical background in aircraft and missile research, development, tooling, maintenance, prototypes, production and electronics. Outstanding attendance and safety records.

## SKILLS & ABILITIES

*SCANS skills*

- Excellent communication skills
- Proven interpersonal skills (teamwork)
- Proven analytical and problem-solving skills
- Certified in air conditioning and refrigerant recovery
- Residential and light commercial electrical wiring skills

## WORK EXPERIENCE

1973-1996     Amax Coal Company                    Chandler, Indiana

Mobile Equipment Operator - Scraper, dozer, endloader, grader, haul truck, crane, etc., and Track Equipment Operator - shovels, dragline (friction and electric), hydraulic excavator.

Welder - Fabricated parts and repairs on all equipment, repaired drills, etc., and performed mechanical maintenance and welding in preparation plant.

Assembly - Built dragline, shovels, and drills in 1973 at the mine (for R. R. Shubert Construction Co.) assisted electricians in wiring equipment.

**Prior to 1973**   Worked in aircraft and missile industry (Phoenix, AZ) as noted in qualifications.

*Summarize the technical background even though it is 23 years*

## CERTIFICATIONS

- E.P.A. Refrigerant Transition & Recovery Certification
- Motor Vehicle Air Conditioning Certification
- CDL License (Class A with tanker, hazardous material, etc.)

## EDUCATION & TRAINING

| | | |
|---|---|---|
| 1994 - 1997 | Ivy Tech State College | Evansville, Indiana |
| | Industrial Technology/HVAC/Electrical Wiring | |
| 1994 - 1997 | P.I.C. Training Center | Boonville, Indiana |
| | Computer Training/Algebra | |
| 1995 - 1996 | North Adult Education | Evansville, Indiana |
| | Vocational/Technical/HVAC/Electricity | |

Previous course work at Arizona State University, Tempe, AZ
Welding/Metalurgy

*Don't do this!*

# Mike Wambach

526 Hillside Drive
Pittsburgh, Pennsylvania
412-653-4482

*Bad appearance*

**References available upon request.** *Too cluttered*

## Career Objective

Professional career in the area of Administration, Purchasing, or Public Relations with an established firm who will utilize my positive attitude, leadership abilities, and communication skills.

## Operations Management

**Electronic Alarms, Inc.**
May 1990 - February 1992: Office Manager

*Looks like a newspaper ad*

Office manager for a corporation specializing in commercial grade closed circuit audio/video systems development, sales, and service. Oversaw the operation of the office and the installation/service departments. Responsibilities included Human Resources, accounting, product and job acquisitions, and systems development and design.

**Human Resource** experience included recruitment, hiring, training, computerized New Hire paperwork processing, benefits setup and administration, policy formulation, HR manuals with job descriptions.

**Accounting** experience included supervising accounts receivable, accounts payable, and payroll clerks.

**Job Acquisition** included supervising credit reporting and leasing department, installation department, and directly involved with job costing analysis.

**Product Acquisitions** included inventory, product quality, delivery scheduling, new vendor recruitment, system design, and troubleshooting technical problems.

**Systems development and design** Position required use of PC based computer systems and software including a customer account information system and telemarketing information systems of my own design.

## Public Relations

**Pittsburgh Specialty Services**

*Hard to read*

October 1988-May 1990: Public Relations and Outside Sales (Seniority based reorganization due to federal budget cutbacks impacting government supported non-profit organizations.)

Primary responsibility for the outside sales of the workshop's client's services, job acquisition, pricing,costing, time and motion studies, supervision of progress and quality control, and customer relations.

Secondary responsibilities included Public Relations, working with area businessmen and political leaders and to be active in the Chamber of Commerce and other business/political organizations. In addition, I handled press conferences and worked with the marketing company. Position required strong leadership and communication skills,

## Management
## McDuff Fast Foods

*Too much use of "I"*

April 1985-October 1988: Assistant Manager

Shift management, scheduling, paperwork. I was the store's designated trainer for hourly employees and new management trainees. I completed 6 week management training in 3 weeks and was promoted to 1st assistant in less than 4 months and was training for General Manager.

## Window Tinting Service

May 1980 - April 1985: General Manager (College employment)

Was responsible for all aspects of business dealing with window tinting and energy management systems and products. Duties included staffing, management, operations, sales, and inventory.

*No white space around the page*

*Too wordy*

*Excellent example*

# Harold J. Morgan, P.E.
2400 S. Burkhardt
Evansville, Indiana 47716
812-478-5111

## PROFESSIONAL PROFILE
Degreed engineer with project management expertise in engineering and light commercial or residential construction with extensive experience in problem-solving and a track record of completing projects on time within established budgets.

## SKILLS & ABILITIES
- Excellent communication skills (oral and written)
- Skilled in strategic planning using analytical and technical skills.
- Experienced in multi-million dollar construction projects
- Experienced in use of Programmable Logic Controllers

## SELECTED ACCOMPLISHMENTS
- Tracked and coordinated materials for construction projects in excess of $10 million
- Reduced cost $2 million annually by linking all remote locations to central office
- Supervised major residential construction program completing 60 homes per year

## PROFESSIONAL EXPERIENCE
**1980 - 1995**          **American Coal Company**          Evansville, Indiana
*Senior Project Engineer*
Tracked and coordinated cost and materials for multi-million dollar construction projects, working on complex projects with limited placement areas, resources and funding. Started as summer student, advancing to Engineering Data Specialist and then Project Engineer.

**1974 - 1979**          **Valley Homes and Construction**  Evansville, Indiana
*Construction Supervisor*
Construction work in light commercial and residential.

## EDUCATION & TRAINING
**Purdue University, 1986**          **University of Southern Indiana, 1978**
West Lafayette, Indiana          Evansville, Indiana
B.S.C.E. Civil Engineering          B.S. Economics and Political Science

Company sponsored training in Management skills, Team building, TQM, etc.

## LICENSE & CERTIFICATION
Professional Engineer
State of Indiana, 1994

# Robert J. Morrison
110 Balmoral Drive
Henderson, Kentucky 50260
502-471-3554

**PROFILE**
Computer programmer with broad-based experience in program development, operations, maintenance, systems analys and design, troubleshooting and repair of equipment.

**SKILLS AND ABILITIES**
- Excellent communication skills (oral and written)
- Team player and ability to work in a multi-cultural environment
- Proven problem-solving and decision-making skills
- Proven organizational skills and detail oriented
- Motivated, self-starter and dependable

**ACCOMPLISHMENTS**
- Functional expansion of product-line maintenance, order processing, and sales history programs for 130 retail store chain operation.
- Design and implementation of procedure to monitor and control access to application source code files.
- Improved efficiency of circulation, advertising, and payroll programs for metropolitan newspaper

**WORK EXPERIENCE**

1991 - 1996      **Record Shop Stores**      Henderson, KY
**Computer Applications Manager**
Application development related to music industry products (CD's, cassettes, etc.), involving inventory maintenance, order processing, sales history, and merchandising for 130 stores.

1990 - 1991      **Evansville Newspapers**      Evansville, IN
**Hardware Technician**
Troubleshoot and repair equipment, such as computer terminals, disk drives, personal computers, etc.

1988 - 1990      **Physicians Health Plan**      Evansville, IN
**Computer Systems Manager**
Responsible for scheduling, maintenance and coordination of user access, system security, system back-ups, and software modiffications.

1979 - 1988      **Evansville, Newspapers**      Evansville, IN
**Computer Applications Manager**
Development, maintenance, enhancement of circulation, advertising and payroll programs in regional newspaper. Involved in new file design, analysis and modification of run-time procedures and disk file replacement to improve performance. Started as operator, promoted in two years to programmer.

**EDUCATION & HONORS**
IVY Tech State College      Evansville, IN
- Associate degree (Electronics Technology)      1992
HONORS - Outstanding Student / GPA 3.557
- Computer courses (night classes)      1981-1982
- Electronics courses (night classes)      1972-1974

# James K. Rasey
115 Wabash Drive
Lexington, Kentucky
606-749-2436

*Very good!*

## PROFILE

Marketing professional with broad-based retail experience, including five years in store management and two years handling merchant credit card contracts, with proficient computer skills, plus training in data management and accounting

## SKILLS & ABILITIES
- Excellent communication skills (oral and written)
- Team player with proven organizational skills
- Proven analytical and problem-solving skills
- Proficient computer skills (WordPerfect, etc.)

## WORK EXPERIENCE

**1990 - 1996**   **Tandy Leather Company**          Lexington, Kentucky
Store Manager
Responsible for overall operation of leather crafts supply store, including hiring and training staff, ordering stock, maintaining inventory, handling advertising and promotions, preparation of sales reports, and all financial records. Started in Evansville (IN) store, promoted to manager in one year, then transferred to Lexington in 1995.

**1984 - 1990**   **Sears Roebuck & Co.**          Evansville, Indiana
Data Entry Clerk
Handled telephone complaints and requests on maintenance agreements, entered data into computer terminal, prepared daily quota sheets for sales personnel, and prepared daily sales reports.

**1982 - 1983**   **American Express Co.** (part-time while in college)   Lexington, Kentucky
Independent Representative (Lexington area)
Signed new merchant credit card contracts, explained procedures, called on existing accounts and handled problems and complaints.

## EDUCATION
**1989**          **Ivy Tech State College**          Evansville, Indiana
Certificate in Information and Data Management (with accounting courses)

**1981 - 1984**   **University of Kentucky**          Lexington, Kentucky
Chemistry and computer science

# Steven E. Wulf
1628 Forest Avenue
St. Louis, MO 43682
616-437-9751

*Excellent!*

## PROFILE
Finance professional with extensive experience in computer engineering and data control plus corporate accounting, administrative budgeting plus project cost analysis, resource analysis, budget comparisons and contract management including regulatory compliance.

## SKILLS & ABILITIES
- Excellent communications skills, both oral and written
- Excellent interpersonal skills, team management and leadership
- Proven analytical and problem solving skills
- Excellent computer skills, (Lotus 1,2,3, WordPerfect, and Windows 95
- Experienced in Critical Path Management and Cost Control Programs
- Self-starter, dependable, performance and detail-oriented

## WORK EXPERIENCE

**1987 - 1995**     **Mid-America Coal Company**     Henderson, Kentucky
Senior Accountant

Started as **Budget Analyst** but was promoted to **Accountant** then **Senior Accountant**. Prepared financial statements, analyzed account balances for accuracy, developed reports for auditors, administered mainframe financial programs, prepared various monthly journal entries, and reviewed invoices with respect to state sales tax laws and audits.

**1973 - 1987**     **Mid-America Coal Company**     St. Louis, Missouri
Construction Accounting Analyst

Started as **Data Control Coordinator** and then **Engineering Technician,** worked directly with Design Engineering and Construction, provided project cost analysis, resource analysis and budget comparisons using Critical Cost Control programs. Designed and managed mainframe database programs to accumulate budget data, designed special reports, recorded acquisitions, liquidated assets and provided administrative support.

## EDUCATION & TRAINING

**1996**     Pinnacle Computer Services, Evansville, Indiana
Novell - CNE Certificate
**1996**     University of Evansville, Evansville, Indiana
Master Microcomputer Certificate
**1973**     St. Louis University, St. Louis, Missouri
Control Data Institute graduate

## David Morrison

1728 Bellemeade     Bedford, OH 47802
601-782-9861

---

### PROFILE

Production Planner with extensive experience in forecasting, scheduling, inventory control and quality assurance plus a solid background in departmental supervision and plant protection including company policy enforcement, fire protection and rescue service, hazardous material procedures, safety training and fire protection.

### SKILLS & ABILITIES

- Excellent communication skills - both written and oral
- Proven analytical and problem-solving skills
- Proven interpersonal skills and team leadership
- Motivated, self-starter, and dependable
- Proficient computer skills (LOTUS, Windows, etc.)

*If space is limit use this altern heading to ke your resu on one page*

### ACCOMPLISHMENTS

- Implemented system to reduce inventory process time by 75%; manpower by 50%
- Redesigned Hot Mill scheduling system to reduce cycle time by 85%
- Reduced Hot Mill flow time and operating inventory
- Created Thermal Department LOTUS spreadsheet to computerize schedules

### WORK EXPERIENCE

**1978 - 1994**          **ALCO Industries**          Louisville, Kentucky
**Production Planner** (1986 - 1993) Projected production forecasts. Established and implemented production scheduling and inventory control procedures. Scheduled maintenance down-time and production crew overtime requirements.

**Plant Protection Officer** (1978 - 1986, 1993) Maintained enforcement of company policies. Controlled ingress and egress. Provided fire protection and rescue servicce and investigated thefts/accidents/fires. Conducted safety training, fire prevention and disaster preparedness program. Conducted plant safety inspection.

**1973 - 1977**          **United States Air Force**          Homestead, Florida
Captain (Security Police) Security alert team leader, assistant flightline area supervisor, and trip coordinator/dispatcher.

### EDUCATION & TRAINING

University of Southern Indiana          Evansville, Indiana
B.S. in Business Administration, 1996

**Company Sponsored Training**
Time Management, Team Building, Personal Diversity, Effective Presentations, Work Relationships, Statistical Analysis, Hazardous Materials, Electrical Hazards, Fire Fighting, E.M.T. and CPR

# Kathleen A. Thomas

930 S. Broad Street • Newburgh, Indiana 47720
812-347-9821

*Alternate heading*

## PROFESSIONAL PROFILE

Employment and training professional with 13 years experience in all phases of case management; from client evaluation and assessment, to career planning and job placement, including eleven years supervision in plant operations and training services for people with barriers to employment.

## SKILLS & ABILITIES

- Excellent communication skills (verbal and written)
- Proven analytical and problem-solving skills (detail oriented)
- Team player with exceptional interpersonal skills
- Ability to interpret and implement federal regulations
- Proficient computer skills (including Microsoft, Windows and WordPerfect)
- Dependable self-starter with proven organizational skills

## WORK EXPERIENCE

1994 - 1997     **Warrick P.I.C. Training Center**     Boonville, IN
Case Manager (Clean Air Project)

Responsible for comprehensive case management including client evaluation and testing, individual assessment, career counseling and planning; vocational training, job development and employer contact, in a Department of Labor funded, four year project to retrain mine workers who were laid off due to federal Clean Air legislation.

1983 - 1994     **Southern Rehabilitation Services, Inc.**     Boonville, IN
Production Coordinator

Supervised all plant operations, related data entry, maintained inventories on materials, and equipment, customer relations and quality asurance; implemented D.O.L. and O.S.H.A. regulations; team leader for production staff, ergonomic advisor, and Safety Director. Coordinated all shipping and receiving. Started as Instructor for disabled adults, promoted to Work Services Supervisor and then Production Coordinator.

## EDUCATION & TRAINING

**University of Evansville**
Liberal Studies Degree Program
1995 -1997

**University of Southern Indiana**
Special Education
1979 - 1981

*Note the example of company sponsored training on these two pages.*

**Company sponsored training:**

Total Quality Management
Self-Directed Work Teams
Ergonomics and Flow Charts
Dealing with Difficult People

Effective Case Management
Sign Language
Behavior Modification
Managing Multiple Priorities

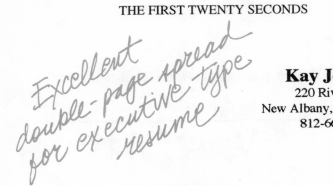

*Excellent double-page spread for executive type resume*

# Kay Johnson
220 River Road
New Albany, Indiana 42251
812-667-0342

## PROFESSIONAL PROFILE

Management professional experienced in development and operation of employment and training programs in a multi-county area, including contract negotiations, program analysis, budgeting, operational procedures, monitoring and technical assistance plus interpretation and implementation of federal and state government regulations. Secretarial and customer service background and accomplished speaker.

## SKILLS & ABILITIES

- Excellent communication skills, both oral and written
- Proven interpersonal skills and team leadership
- Excellent organization skills and detail oriented
- Proven analytical and problem solving skills
- Proficient computer skills, (WordPerfect, Lotus, Word, etc.)
- Ability to interpret and implement government regulations

## SELECTED ACHIEVEMENTS

- Developed a contract monitoring and performance review system accepted as a model for the State of Indiana
- Facilitated the start-up of computerized literacy laboratories in five county offices
- Guided the development of a comprehensive customer assessment system which has improved the development of individualized training plans for customers

## EDUCATION & DEGREES

**1995 - Masters Degree in Public Administration** - Human Resources Developmen'
Indiana State University, Terre Haute, Indiana

**1984 - Bachelor of Science - Business Marketing and Management**
Indiana University, Bloomington, Indiana

## COMMUNITY ACTIVITIES

**United Way of Central Indiana**
Member: Allocations Committee (1995 and 1996)
Outcomes Committee (1996)

**Girl Scouts of America (1991 - 1997)**
Junior Troop Leader, Brownie Troop Leader

**Step Ahead Council (1994 - 1997)**

## PROFESSIONAL WORK EXPERIENCE

**1988 - 1997  Private Industry Council of Central Indiana, Inc.**   Indianapolis, Indiana

**Contract Manager (1990 - 1997)**  Negotiate, write and monitor contracts in five county area. Developed contract monitoring and performance review system recognized as model for the state. Lead in development of innovative programming. Facilitated effective transition of service delivery revisions required by legislative mandates. Provided technical assistance, performed intensive monitoring and program analysis, revised standard operating procedures that resulted in the organization achieving or exceeding all performance standards for three consecutive years. Work with a board of business and community leaders, lead meeting, and plan events. Coordinate business/education partnership activities.

**Employer Representative (Greenfield office 1988-1990)**  Promoted programs of the Marion County Job Center to employers, agencies and potential customers. Developed and implemented public relations events and outreach programs. Organized and promoted training seminar. Met and exceeded all performance goals, increased exposure of the program by using innovative marketing techniques, designed monthly publication, wrote promotional material, made presentations and worked with media. Interviewed customers to determine their skills and abilities to match personnel needs of employers.

**1986 - 1988      Kelly Temporary Services and Manpower**       Terre Haute, Indiana
**Secretary assignments at Eli Lilly & Consolidated Grain & Barge**
Calculated sales reports, worked with government contracts, used Display Write and Lotus 1-2-3 software. Prepared daily position reports and worked with accounts payable, payroll, etc.

**1985 - 1986      CrediThrift Corp**                New Albany, Indiana
**Collection Specialist and Customer Service Representative.** Answered inquiries, resolved credit card problems. Top performer in processing customer calls. Placed in charge of re-organizing the recoveries collection area. Implemented system to process bankrupt, deceased and charged-off VISA accounts.

## RELATED TRAINING

Numerous workshops, conferences, and seminars with continual training in case management, counseling, team building, functional/contextual instruction, job development marketing, TQM, personal and corporate strategic planning plus program design and management.

## PROFESSIONAL ORGANIZATIONS

National Association of Workforce Development Professionals
American Society of Public Administrators

*Use professional organizations or affiliations when possible*

# Resumes & Facts for High School Students

## Welcome to the Business World

Sooner or later you will need a resume. Now is the time for you to acquaint yourself with what it is, what it does, and how to prepare one.

This book was written primarily for college graduates or experienced workers who are changing careers or who have lost their jobs, but it can be very useful to help you develop your portfolio and write your first resume. You may need one sooner than you think.

When you graduate you will decide on going to college, (technical school, etc.), entering the workforce, or maybe both. Therefore, you need to develop a portfolio of your skills, work experience and accomplishments during high school for the basis of your first resume.

## Competition for jobs

The workplace is changing faster than ever. You need as much education and training as possible. If you enter the work force after high school, you face competition from college graduates with more education and experienced workers with more training. There are many more applicants than there are jobs.

Surveys show that employers spend less than 20 seconds scanning a resume to decide whether to read it, so your resume must generate interest on the first glance.

Review the three steps to develop an effective resume. COMPILE your information, ANALYZE your information, and ORGANIZE your information (pages 7-10-16) using action words to SELL YOUR SKILLS!

Start now to compile information about your skills, capabilities and accomplishments. Most of all, get as much education and training as possible to compete in the workplace.

## What employers want! Sell your skills!

Numerous surveys about what employers expect in employees have been published in the last few years. Virtually all of them reached similar conclusions. Employers want employees to have better skills to meet the demands of the high-performance high-tech workplace.

These skills were identified in the U.S. Dept. of Labor 1992 SCANS Report as the Foundation Skills and the Five Workplace Competencies (page 11 - 12).

Even though this information is on the page about "What employers expect", we place special emphasis on it for students and new graduates to have these skills - the BASIC skills, the THINKING skills, and the PERSONAL QUALITIES.

Unfortunately, many applicants, including new graduates entering the workforce do not possess these skills. Therefore, applicants who do possess them stand out way above the rest.

So review the SCANS report to determine which skills you have and which ones need improvement. Then show them on your resume and SELL YOURSELF!

## Matthew Smith

1201 First Street
Boonville, Indiana 47601
812-897-9881

*this approach can also be used for college students*

## PROFILE & OBJECTIVE

Energetic high school student with training in computer technology and above average math scores looking for summer employment or internship in healthcare field

*A new high school graduate resume is on page 38*

## SKILLS & ABILITIES

- Excellent communication skills (oral and written)
- Proficient computer skills (WordPerfect, Windows, etc.)
- Exceptional math skills (4.0 grade level)
- Proven analytical and problem solving skills
- Self-starter, motivated, and dependable
- Ability to organize and complete projects

## WORK EXPERIENCE

1995 - 1996        ABC Warehouse                Boonville, Indiana
                   Warehouse Clerk (summer work)

General warehouse duties including shipping and receiving, inventory, pricing, and stocking

1994 - 1995        Warrick County Fair          Boonville, Indiana
                   Field Crew, Admissions

Took tickets, balanced monies, worked concession stands, etc. (as needed)

## EDUCATION & TRAINING

Boonville High School                              Boonville, Indiana
Major: Double major in science and math
May 1998 - projected graduation date

## SCHOOL ACTIVITIES

*Note the school activities*

Boonville Math Club
Boonville Science Club
Boonville Marching Band

# Facts for College Students

If you didn't start your portfolio in high school, then do it now. You need as much information as possible about your skills, work experience, and accomplishments to prepare an effective resume.

The following suggestions will help you.

**1. REVIEW EMPLOYMENT OPPORTUNITIES.** Think about your occupational interests, your capabilities, your likes and dislikes, and then research the employment opportunities in the fields of your choice. The books listed below contain detailed information about virtually all industries, employment outlook and more. Your college Career/Placement Office can also give you guidance.

**2. LEARN BUSINESS TERMINOLOGY.** Review the information in these books to familiarize yourself with business terminology used in job descriptions, etc. Study them. This will help you when writing your resume and during interviews with employers.

**3. BUILD EXPERIENCE.** If possible, involve yourself in college activities related to your career choice. Opportunities such as the college newspaper, radio station, business office, departmental affairs, etc. to gain experience. Contact local businesses such as banks or retail stores regarding part-time employment. You can also contact the chamber of commerce for a list of voluntary organizations, many of which are glad to have college students help out.

**4. KEEP GOOD RECORDS.** Keep a running log of your activities and accomplishments with thorough explanations so you can use this information when you prepare your resume.

**5. REVIEW.** This book contains virtually all the information you need to prepare an effective resume with excellent examples to follow. Your work experience and accomplishments in college will make your resume stand out above the rest.

**CAREER GUIDE TO AMERICA'S TOP INDUSTRIES.** Covers trends and opportunities in 450 major industries with details about types of jobs available.

**AMERICA'S TOP JOBS FOR COLLEGE GRADUATES.** Contains descriptions for 60 of the top jobs held by college graduates with summary information on an additional 500 jobs.

**AMERICA'S 50 FASTEST GROWING JOBS.** Provides descriptions on jobs with the fastest growth rate.

**AMERICA'S TOP 300 JOBS.** Contains descriptions of 250 occupations with earnings potential, future outlook and related occupations.

**AMERICA'S TOP TECHNICAL & TRADE JOBS.** Contains descriptions for more than 50 of the top technical and trade jobs with summary information on more than 500 jobs that require technical skills but don't require a college degree.

The references mentioned above may be available at your public library, and all can be purchased from JIST Works, Inc. 720 North Park Avenue, Indianapolis, IN 46202. Phone: 317-264-3720

# Stephanie Smith
R.R. 1, Box 22
Rockport, IN 47637
812-236-7328

*Excellent resume*

## PROFILE & OBJECTIVE
Energetic college senior with excellent organizational and interpersonal skills pursuing career in research and development, quality assurance and/or statistical process control fields

## SKILLS & ABILITIES
- Excellent communication skills (oral and written)
- Excellent planning and organizational skills
- Excellent interpersonal and public relations skills
- Excellent problem-solving skills & detail oriented

## WORK EXPERIENCE

| | | |
|---|---|---|
| 1992 - 1995 (Fall/Spring) | **Western Kentucky University Police Dept.** Records Clerk (student employee) | Bowling Green, KY |

Organized data and entered in computer system, filed hard copies, processed paperwork, and collected money for citations and reports. Handled conflicts with customers plus participated in public relations program including a film production.

| | | |
|---|---|---|
| Spring 1994 | **Mediplex Rehabilitation Center** Recreational Volunteer | Bowling Green, KY |

Assisted patients with activities, motivated unwilling and reluctant patients to participate. Also listened to patient needs and concerns and communicated problems to Center staff. Received volunteer of month recognition.

| | | |
|---|---|---|
| 1991 - 1995 (Summers) | **Hardee's Restaurant** Cashier/Clerk | Owensboro, KY |

Worked cash drawer during opening shift, organized and cleaned work area, other duties as needed.

## EDUCATION & CERTIFICATION

**Western Kentucky University**                                     Bowling Green, KY
Bachelor of Science
May 1996 (projected)
Major: Biology
Minor: Chemistry/Psychology

- CPR Certified
- Basic First Aid Knowledge

*The part-time work really enhances her resume*

*Excellent resume for high school graduate*

# Marlene Jefferson

1624 Westwood Drive
Louisvillele, Kentucky 40504
502-582-1118

## PROFILE & OBJECTIVE

Energetic high school graduate with excellent communication, organizational
and interpersonal skills pursuing career in specialty or technical marketing

## SKILLS & ABILITIES

- Excellent communication skills (verbal and written)
- Detail oriented with proven organizational skills
- Excellent interpersonal and public relations skills
- Analytical and problem-solving skills
- Self starter, dependable and efficient

## ACCOMPLISHMENTS

- Four years 4.0 GPA
- First place in Reynolds Scholarship Contest
- First place winner in Science Fair 1997
- President of Senior Class 1997

## WORK EXPERIENCE (while attending school)

1994 - 1995    Jefferson School Corp. office Louisville, KY
(summers)      Records Clerk (student employee)
               Organized data, processed paperwork, entered data into
               computer system, etc.

1994 - 1996    Hardee's Restaurant          St. Matthews, KY
(weekends)     Cashier/Clerk
               Worked cash drawer, practiced suggestive sales, organized
               and cleaned work area, other duties as needed

19923 - 1994   Jefferson Cadet              Louisville, KY
(weekends)     Reporter
               Reported school news and wrote articles for school paper

## EDUCATION & TRAINING

Louisville Central High School          Louisville, KY
Graduated May 1996 - Double Major in Science and Math

Sales Training at Hardee's

## Elizabeth J. Young
2263 East Riverside
Sandusky, Ohio 68213
419-869-4523

*Excellent resume*

### PROFILE & OBJECTIVE
Energetic college graduate with banking experience and training in advertising. Pursuing career in marketing, public relations, or related work in a financial institution.

### SKILLS & ABILITIES

- Excellent communication skills (oral and written)
- Proven interpersonal skills (team work)
- Ability to work in a multi-cultural environment
- Detail oriented and good organizational skills
- Proficient computer skills (Lotus, Windows95, etc.)

### ACCOMPLISHMENTS AND HONORS
- Participated in National Advertising Contest Competition with 20 other colleges. Ball State team placed 2nd in overall competition. First time Ball State had ever taken part in this national competition.
- Muncie Advertising Club Scholarship Recipient 1991-1994
- Rotary Club Scholarship Recipient 1991-1994
- Dean's List 1991-1994
- Graduated summa cum laude

### WORK EXPERIENCE
MUNCIE STATE BANK
**Bank Teller**    1994 (part-time while in college)
Part-time teller at the east side branch. Handled deposits, withdrawals and cashing checks. Balanced drawer daily.

*Her part-time work is related to her career!*

BALL STATE UNIVERSITY    MUNCIE, INDIANA
**Student Secretary** - Admissions Office    1993
Processed applications for admission and did general clerical work for departmental Vice-President.

BALL STATE UNIVERSITY    MUNCIE, INDIANA
**Student Intern**    1992-1994
Compiled research information for various projects and entered data into computer.

### EDUCATION
Ball State University, Muncie, Indiana    1994
B.S. Degree in Marketing & Business Administration
Minors in Psychology and Advertising

# For Women Only...
# From Mommy Track to Career Track
## (or Family Management to Career Management)

Many women have a serious problem when trying to enter or re-enter the workforce after raising a family.

The employer thinks you didn't do anything as a housewife, you've been out of touch too long or you don't have any skills that are usable.

Nothing could be further from the truth!

*this is actual work that requires skills*

How in the world does that employer think you managed the family finances, worked in the PTA and Girl Scouts, taught in the Sunday School, counseled your teenagers, worked on fund drives, did all kinds of volunteer work, tried to look like a movie star for your husband, and cleaned the house, all under the heading of housewife, without any skills?

BE REAL - the employer didn't have this many problems and he was paid a nice fat salary.

Many job consultants recommend that you show your volunteer work on your resume. And you should. But many employers don't want to admit skills in volunteer work are transferable to the workplace.

Therefore, what you say and how you say it will determine whether you get past the scrutiny of that employer who thinks you don't have any skills or not enough experience.

Review the SCANS skills (pages 11 and 12) and the resume on the next page. Think about how many skills you used in your volunteer work that are used in the workplace and put them in your resume, but do it so they enhance your experience.

Normally, volunteer work shown under the heading of "COMMUNITY INVOLVEMENT" is a plus factor when the resume has adequate work history. But many employers have a tendency to overlook skills used in volunteer organization work when you have limited work history in the private sector.

The best way to overcome this situation is to emphasize the importance of those organization skills relative to the workplace. Remember that many of those skills are identical to skills used in the workplace.

*make a list of your skills*

So evaluate all the skills you used in volunteer organizations, fund drives, PTA, Girl Scouts, etc. and build a section for organization work showing offices held, responsibilities, and accomplishments.

Include this information when you summarize your experience in your PROFILE.

Give your PROFILE a new perspective and convince the employer that you do have the qualifications and experience for the job.

The following resume actually resulted in an interview and employment because the PROFILE enhanced her experience by combining the time spent in volunteer organization work with the time spent in the workplace.

The employer interviewed her and she was hired.

*Bonnie did it — you can too!*

# Bonnie Harmon
5026 Washington Avenue
Evansville, IN 47715
812-977-1275

*Combine your organization work with private sector employment*

## PROFESSIONAL PROFILE

Management professional with extensive experience working with youth and adults in counseling, individual assessment, career development, and organization work including five years experience helping dislocated workers with retraining and placement assistance. Rapid advancement to supervision of $1.3 million training project plus fifteen years community organization work. Interested in college level career counseling or similar position in private sector.

## ADMINISTRATIVE SKILLS & ABILITIES

- Excellent communication skills (both written and oral)
- Proven analytical and problem solving skills (critical thinking)
- Outstanding organizational skills and detail oriented
- Ability to develop and implement marketing and recruitment programs
- Proven track record in career counseling and job placement
- Excellent interpersonal skills, team player, and diplomatic ability
- Excellent computer skills including DOS, Windows, WordPerfect, Lotus 123

*Emphasis on SCANS skills*

## PROFESSIONAL EXPERIENCE

1991-1996    **Private Industry Council/Job Training Center**    Boonville and Evansville, IN
Supervisor - Clean Air Project (1994-1996)

Organized and implemented $1.3 million program to retrain workers in the coal mining industry who were terminated because of the federal Clean Air Act. Responsible for recruitment, career counseling, retraining and placement of miners including eligibility requirements and documentation according to federal and state regulations. Previously worked as Job Developer to counsel dislocated workers, conduct assessment and evaluation, determine occupational interests and potential in order to develop employability plan and arrange training. Also worked as youth counselor in summer program

1976 - 1991    **Organizational Experience**    Evansville, IN

Coach - Soccer & Tennis (1976-1989)  Coached teen girls soccer and tennis teams in two city leagues, responsible for organizing, scheduling, counseling, solving problems, motivating players and crisis intervention.

Program Chairman - Medical Society Auxiliary  - Planned, organized and arranged monthly meetings. Responsible for programs.

Note - also worked on fund drives for social agencies, managed household affairs, and raised family, served as Brownie Leader, Den Mother (Girl Scouts)

*Transferrable skills are important!*

## EDUCATION & TRAINING

Dale Carnegie Training                                          1995
Western Kentucky University    Master of Arts in Education    1994
University of Evansville    Bachelor of Liberal Studies    1991

# How To Write Your Cover Letter

You **must** send a cover letter with every resume. The way you write your cover letter is just as important as the way you wrote your resume.

Think of your cover letter as your introduction to the employer and the impact it will have on his first impression of you. It will either enhance the FIRST TWENTY SECONDS or it will detract from the FIRST TWENTY SECONDS.

Cover letters should be exactly that, a one-page cover introducing your resume. Most job search consultants agree that the ideal cover letter should have three paragraphs or parts and no more.

**Part One.** Why are you sending a resume? What ad are you answering, who referred you to the company, how you knew the company was expanding, or other research you had done on the company or any other reason you might have to send your resume to the particular company.

**Part Two.** Why the company should hire you. Such as, emphasizing how

your experience meets the job requirements, your training is transferable to the company needs or how your accomplishments show potential value to the company. Refer to your resume. **But don't repeat your job description. This is your chance to emphasize why you are the right applicant for the job. Sell yourself!**

**Part Three.** Ask for a response. No sales presentation is complete and no sale is ever made unless the sales person asks for the order.

However, this is the most sophisticated sale you will ever make so use finesse in what you say and how you say it. **But you must ask!**

The cover letter examples show how you express an interest in a personal interview followed with a question about when it would be possible, in an attempt to solicit an answer. The employer has to at least think about it. **Finalize the letter with a comment about how you will make the next contact.**

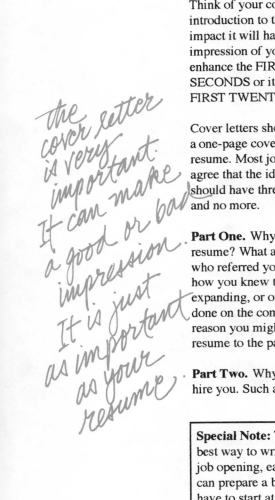

*the cover letter is very important. It can make a good or bad impression. It is just as important as your resume*

---

**Special Note:** The above instructions show you what most experts agree is the best way to write a cover letter. Since each cover letter is written for a specific job opening, each should be individualized for that purpose. However, you can prepare a basic core of information as shown in the examples. You won't have to start at the beginning each time. Vary the letters by emphasizing what is most applicable in each case. This will make it easier when you are sending out a number of resumes. **Remember, every resume must have a cover letter.**

A similar situation applies to resumes. When you consider employment in two different fields, you may need two versions of your resume. This is easily accomplished by changing the emphasis in your PROFILE, ACCOMPLISHMENTS, TRAINING, and WORK EXPERIENCE accordingly. But you don't have to write a complete new resume.

# Do's and Don'ts for Cover Letters

**Do's**

Many of the Do's and Don'ts for cover letters are the same or similar to those for resumes. However, because they're so important for you, we'll list them anyway.

• Make sure your cover letter is neat and pleasing to the eye with enough border and white space so it's similar to your resume.

• Use paper that matches your resume if possible. Or use a high quality bond typing paper.

• Be sure to type your cover letter or do it on a computer if your resume is computer done.

• Keep your cover letter brief, on one page. But include enough information in the second paragraph about why they should hire you so they will be sure to read your resume.

• Take the initiative! Tell the employer that you will call him about an interview appointment. If you tell him Tuesday, make sure you make that call on Tuesday. Not on Wednesday or Thursday.

**Don'ts**

• Don't clutter the page. Keep plenty of white space around the body of the cover letter.

• Don't use inferior paper that detracts from your cover letter and your resume.

• Don't write your cover letter in longhand. Find someone with either a typewriter or a computer.

• Don't use a typewriter with a script typeface. Keep the executive look.

• Don't expect the employer to call you. They won't. They may have 200 resumes to sift through about the same job. They do not have time to acknowledge every resume they receive. They will only contact the ones that interest them.

• Don't write two-page cover letters. They will be too long, too wordy, and too much trouble to read. Remember the TWENTY SECOND Rule.

• Don't use a P.O. Box unless you also include your address.

---

**IMPORTANT:** When you write cover letters (and resumes), be sure to proofread them and correct any errors. **But there is more...** read them and review them AGAIN, AGAIN, AGAIN and AGAIN to make sure they look professional, they are accurate, they are factual, and they convey what you mean to the employer. It's your future that is on the line.

Address your cover letter to a specific individual if possible. If you don't have a name, then send them to specific management personnel such as President, Vice-President of Engineering, etc.

## EXAMPLE OF COVER LETTER RESPONDING TO AN AD

2625 Northwoods Court
Cincinnati, Ohio 21662
October 10, 1994

Mr. Robert H. Miller
Vice-President of Engineering
American Information Systems
Newark, New Jersey 10631

Dear Mr. Miller,

I am very much interested in the Manufacturing Engineer position in your advertisement in today's issue of the *Wall Street Journal*. A copy of my resume is enclosed.

*He is selling experience relative to the new job.*

Please note that I have eleven years experience using AutoCAD to design injection-molded and vacuum-formed plastic parts which are comparable to AIS products. Since your company does business overseas, also note, that I have made several trips to vendors in the Pacific Rim to offer technical assistance.

Enclosed is my salary history but that is not the primary consideration. I am sure your salary structure is commensurate with the job responsibilities and I would appreciate a personal interview to discuss the job opening in detail. Would it be possible to meet with you next week? I will call your secretary to find out if this is convenient for you and to establish a time. Thanks for your consideration.

*Handling the sala[ry] question*

*Or you could say "I will call you to find out if this is convenient."*

Sincerely,

David Morrison

## EXAMPLE OF COVER LETTER FROM
## PERSONAL REFERRAL

2625 Northwoods Court
Cincinnati, Ohio 21662
October 10, 1994

Mr. Robert Miller
Vice-President of Engineering
American Information Systems
Newark, New Jersey 10631

Dear Mr. Miller,

Mr. Charles Sawyer of Angst Anvil said you were looking for a Manufacturing Engineer with my experience and suggested I send you my resume.

Please note that I have eleven years experience in designing injection-molded and vacuum-formed plastic parts similar to products that your company manufactures. In addition, I am proficient in the use of AutoCad.

I would appreciate a personal interview to discuss potential employment with your firm. Would it be possible to meet with you next week? I will call your secretary to see if this would be agreeable with you. Thank you for your consideration.

*Asking for an interview*

Sincerely,

David Morrison

*Or you could say "I will call you to see if this would be agreeable."*

## EXAMPLE OF COVER LETTER FOR DIRECT CONTACT
## AFTER RESEARCH ABOUT COMPANY

2625 Northwoods Court
Cincinnati, Ohio 21662
October 10, 1994

Mr. Robert H. Miller
Vice-President of Engineering
American Information Systems
Newark, New Jersey 10631

Dear Mr. Miller,

I have been researching plastics manufacturing firms and noticed that your company announced a five-year expansion program. I am interested in a position in your design department and have enclosed my resume.

Please note that I have eleven years experience in designing injection-molded and vacuum-formed plastic parts similar to those produced by your company. In addition, I am proficient in the use of AutoCad.

I would appreciate a personal interview to discuss potential employment with your firm. I have enclosed a Quik-Response form with a self addressed, stamped envelope for your convenience. Would it be possible to meet with you next week? I will call your secretary to see if this would be agreeable.

Thank you for your consideration.

Sincerely,

David Morrison

David Morrison

*the Quik Response form is included in "Better Job Search in 3 Easy Steps"*

## EXAMPLE OF COVER LETTER FOR
## NEW COLLEGE GRADUATE

2263 East Riverside
Sandusky, Ohio 68213
October 11, 1994

Mr. Charles Worth
Vice-President, Marketing & Public Relations
Hoosier Financial Services
2000 N. Meridian Street
Indianapolis, Indiana 46204

Dear Mr. Worth,

Your annual report shows a consistent growth during *She included information about the bank.* the past five years with the addition of ten new branches. I am interested in a position in your marketing department and have enclosed a copy of my resume.

I have just graduated from Ball State University with a degree in Marketing and Business Administration. I have worked part-time during my senior year as a bank teller to gain valuable experience, as noted on my resume. In addition, my special training includes psychology, advertising, and computer technology. I would be willing and pleased to go through any training programs your company offers.

*Emphasis on her part-time work is important.*

I would appreciate a personal interview to discuss my qualifications and potential employment. Would it be possible to meet with you next week to discuss my situation? I will call your secretary to see if this would be convenient for you.

Thanks for your consideration.

Sincerely,
Elizabeth Young
Elizabeth Young

*Or you could say "I will call you to see if this would be convenient."*

## Suggested Sources of Occupational Information for the Job Seeker

Information about most occupations with job descriptions, employment outlook, etc., is available in virtually all public libraries in their reference sections. Copies of some references may be ordered from the U.S. Government Printing Office or from other suppliers. A partial list of the most popular books follows.

**Occupational Outlook Handbook,** published by the U.S. Department of Labor. Possibly the best general reference available - it contains descriptions of the 250 occupations in which most Americans are employed. Updated every two years, the descriptions include nature of work, earnings, employment projections, and more.

**Occupational Outlook Quarterly,** U. S. Department of Labor, Bureau of Labor Statistics. A quarterly publication with informative articles about changes in the labor market and updated employment projections for many occupations.

**Dictionary of Occupational Titles,** also published by the U.S. Department of Labor. The "DOT" lists and classifies about 12,741 occupations. The descriptions are very specific, the book includes many jobs that very few people hold, and this book is best used by job seekers and career changers in tandem with either of the following books.

**Complete Guide for Occupational Exploration,** published by JIST Works, Inc. Includes and cross-references all 12,741 job titles from the "DOT" (above), but the titles are clustered into twelve, easy-to-understand interest areas. The interest areas are further divided in such a way that job seekers and career changers can start with their personal interests and find lists of jobs they should explore.

**Enhanced Guide For Occupational Exploration,** published by JIST Works, Inc. Includes and cross-references the 2,500 most important job titles from the "DOT", also organized around twelve, easy-to-understand interest areas. Each listing includes a specific description along with codes that yield insights into work environment, stress factors, aptitudes, physical demands, and much more.

Also available from JIST Works, Inc. is a series of nine targeted career reference books including America's Top 300 Jobs, America's Fifty Fastest Growing Jobs, America's Top Trade and Technical Jobs, and more.

All the references mentioned here may be available at your public library, and all can be purchased from JIST Works, Inc. 720 North Park Avenue, Indianapolis, IN 46202. Phone: 317-264-3720.

# Employment Outlook

The U.S. Government in 1991 published projections (1990 - 2005) for the fastest growing occupations requiring post secondary education and declining occupations during that same period. A partial list is presented for your information This gives you an idea of the rapid changes occurring in the workplace.

**Fastest growing occupations requiring a college degree of major education** (percent of growth)

| | |
|---|---|
| Systems analysts | 79 |
| Computer programmers | 56 |
| Management analysts | 52 |
| Marketing, advertising/PR | 47 |
| Teachers, preschool | 41 |
| Teachers, special ed | 40 |
| Financial services sales | 40 |
| Accountants & auditors | 34 |
| Social workers | 34 |
| Engineering, mathematics | 34 |
| Teachers, secondary | 34 |

Of the 20 fastest growing occupations requiring a bachelor's degree or more education, the top seven are tied to the health services industry or computer technology.

**Fastest growing occupations requiring some postsecondary training or extensive employer training** (percent growth)

| | |
|---|---|
| Paralegals | 85 |
| Medical assistants | 74 |
| Radiologic technicians | 70 |
| Data process equip. repair | 60 |
| Medical records technicians | 54 |
| Electromedical equip. repair | 51 |
| Legal secretaries | 47 |
| Registered nurses | 44 |
| Licensed practical nurses | 42 |
| Dental hygienists | 41 |

Health services occupations are a sizable proportion of the fastest growing occupations requiring some postsecondary training or extensive employer training.

**Occupations with the greatest declines in numbers of people** (thousands)

| | |
|---|---|
| Bookeeping, accounting, auditing clerks | 133 |
| Sewing machine operators | 116 |
| Electrical & electronic assemblers | 105 |
| Typists/word processors | 103 |
| Electric equip. assemblers | 81 |
| Telephone/TV install/repair | 40 |
| Statistical clerks | 31 |
| Bank tellers | 25 |
| Service station attendants | 17 |
| Meter readers, utilities | 12 |

Occupations with the greatest declines in employment are tied to manufacturing or result from technological changes now going on in the workplace.

*Source: Occupational Outlook 1990 - 2005*
*U.S. Department of Labor    Fall 1991*

---

U.S. News & World Report (October 28, 1996) published a feature article about the 20 Hot Job Tracks, which confirms the Department of Labor projections. The following opportunities from the 1991 U.S. News report are on the list of fastest growing occupations:

- Accounting
- Education
- Finance
- Human services
- Technical services
- Advertising
- Engineering
- Healthcare
- Sales

# Computer Disk Instructions

**IBM & Compatible** This disk has all the resumes, cover letters, and worksheets, in the following word processing programs:

| Program / Version | In The Directory Called |
|---|---|
| Lotus AmiPro 3.0 for Windows | amipro.30w |
| Microsoft Word for Windows 2.0 | msword.20w |
| Microsoft Works for Windows 3.0 | msworks.30w |
| WordPerfect 5.0/5.1 for DOS | wordperf.51d |
| WordPerfect 6.0/6.1 for Windows | wordperf.61w |

Should you be using an older word processing program than those listed, you might need to upgrade in order to use the disk.

*All trademarks and registered trademarks are the property of their respective holder.*

**1.** Place the disk in your 3.5" drive and start your word processing program. Select the disk drive A or B as the source of the documents. You will see a directory listing with the above directories.

**2.** Call up the resume document layout you like and type in your own information.

**3.** Be sure to spell-check your completed resume and print it out for proofreading. Remember, you **MUST match the visual look** of the resume printed in this book. That will make your resume more effective, easier to read and be the one that makes it through those first 20 Seconds of scrutiny by the employer.

**4.** The disk is write-protected in order to prevent accidentally overwriting the original documents. We recommend that you **do not record** your modified resumes on this disk but rather record them on another disk or on your hard drive.

**5.** If you have an older word processor than the versions listed above, you might try using the wordperf.51d documents as your program **might** convert them.

**6.** You might want to copy the documents from the diskettes directory into a document directory on your hard disk for easier, faster access.

**Macintosh Computers.** If you need a MAC disk, please phone 1-800-977-9332. We'll be happy to send you one. It's in ClarisWorks 2.0.

# About the Authors of this book . . .

**Ben T. Field** is a successful public relations executive with 35 years experience in Marketing, Advertising and Public Relations, including supervisory experience with extensive training and development responsibilities. He has been Art Director at Bristol Myers, Eli Lilly and CIBA/Geigy. Presently, he is a Professional Marketing Consultant under the name Field Design Group.

He is a graduate of the University of Louisville and holds an MFA degree in Graphic Design from Yale University. He has taught creative art and graphic design at the University of Evansville and IVY Tech State College.

**Paul K. Wright**, retired bank vice-president (Industrial Relations), has 35 years experience in business development including 11 years as a Chamber of Commerce executive in economic development and 14 years as a bank executive responsible for industrial relations. The past 11 years he was director of an employment and training center.

Wright studied engineering at Akron University, is a graduate of the Industrial Development Institute at the University of Oklahoma, the Chamber of Commerce Management Institute at the University of Georgia. He has conducted numerous workshops, seminars and sales training sessions.

**OTHER PUBLICATIONS:** Better Job Search In 3 Easy Steps (1997)
Better Job Skills In 3 Easy Steps (1998)